Searchlight BOOKS™

Climate Change

Climate Change and

Air Quality

Linda Crotta Brennan

Lerner Publications ◆ Minneapolis

For Jacob, Anna, Emily, and baby Stith

Lerner Publications Company
A division of Lerner Publishing Group, Inc.
241 First Avenue North
Minneapolis, MN 55401 USA

For reading levels and more information, look up this title at www.lernerbooks.com.

Main body text set in Adrianna Regular 14/20.
Typeface provided by Chank.

Library of Congress Cataloging-in-Publication Data

Names: Brennan, Linda Crotta, author.
Title: Climate change and air quality / by Linda Crotta Brennan.
Description: Minneapolis : Lerner Publications, [2019] | Series: Searchlight books.
    Climate change | Audience: Age 8–11. | Audience: Grade 4 to 6. | Includes
    bibliographical references and index.
Identifiers: LCCN 2018014510 (print) | LCCN 2018023475 (ebook) |
    ISBN 9781541543645 (eb pdf) | ISBN 9781541538641 (lb : alk. paper) |
    ISBN 9781541545892 (pb : alk. paper)
Subjects: LCSH: Climatic changes—Juvenile literature. | Air quality—Juvenile literature.
Classification: LCC QC903.15 (ebook) | LCC QC903.15 .B74 2019 (print) |
    DDC 363.739/2--dc23

LC record available at https://lccn.loc.gov/2018014510

Manufactured in the United States of America
1-45047-35874-6/1/2018

Contents

Chapter 1

FUELING CHANGE

For most of human history, people depended on natural sources for energy, such as animal power, wind power, wood power, and waterpower. If you needed to get from one place to another, you walked. To travel long distances, you rode a horse or sailed with the wind. If you were cold, you burned wood. Waterwheels ground your wheat and powered your factories.

People once depended on strong animals like horses to help with farming.

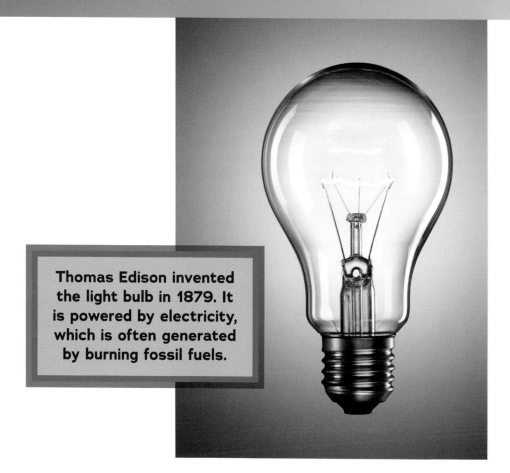

Thomas Edison invented the light bulb in 1879. It is powered by electricity, which is often generated by burning fossil fuels.

Fossil Fuels

By the mid-eighteenth century, many people had switched to fossil fuels for energy. Coal, oil, and natural gas are all fossil fuels. They come from the fossilized remains of ancient plants and animals.

Fossil fuels provided cheaper, more powerful energy. Use of fossil fuels led to the invention of new technology. New inventions such as the light bulb and the internal combustion engine launched an industrial revolution that changed people's lives.

Hurricane Harvey hit Texas in August 2017. Due to climate change, storms like hurricanes are getting stronger.

A Changing Climate

But as our sources of energy changed, Earth's climate began to change too. Climate change is what happens when a place's weather patterns change over time. This includes changes in average heat, rainfall, and wind patterns. Earth's climate is changing right now, and the effects of climate change are getting worse. Temperatures are rising. Storms are getting stronger. Polar ice is melting.

But what is causing climate change? One factor is the decreasing air quality of Earth's atmosphere.

Chapter 2

OUR AIR AFFECTS OUR CLIMATE

Fossil fuels power our cars, heat our homes, run our factories, and generate electricity. Fossil fuels are burned to produce energy. When they burn, fossil fuels give off greenhouse gases.

At this power plant, exhaust from burning fossil fuels pours greenhouse gases into the air.

GREENHOUSE GASES WARM EARTH IN A PROCESS CALLED THE GREENHOUSE EFFECT.

▼

Greenhouse Gases

Greenhouse gases act like the glass of a greenhouse. In a greenhouse, glass lets sunlight through but stops heat from escaping. This heat keeps the greenhouse warm enough for plants to grow even in the winter. Greenhouse gases work in a similar way. During the day, sunlight warms Earth. At night, most of that heat escapes into space. But greenhouse gases trap some of it.

A certain amount of greenhouse gas is good. If all the sun's heat left Earth at night, Earth would be too cold for life to thrive. But when too much greenhouse gas is added to the atmosphere, too much of the sun's heat is trapped. Then Earth's temperature rises higher and higher.

If Earth gets too hot, plants and animals will have trouble getting the water they need to survive.

Carbon Dioxide

The atmosphere contains different kinds of greenhouse gases. The most abundant is carbon dioxide. It is made of one carbon and two oxygen atoms. In the United States, carbon dioxide makes up more than 80 percent of our greenhouse gases. The exhaust from cars, buses, and planes adds a lot of carbon dioxide to the air. Humans add even more carbon dioxide to the atmosphere by burning fossil fuels in power plants and factories.

One car puts about 5 tons (4.5 t) of carbon dioxide into the air each year!

Livestock such as cows release methane when they pass gas.

Methane

Methane is another greenhouse gas. It contains one carbon atom and four hydrogen atoms. Methane makes up only 9 percent of our greenhouse gases, but it is more powerful than carbon dioxide. It can hold over twenty times more heat. Methane leaks into the air during the production of fossil fuels. It bubbles up from our rotting landfills. It's given off by farm animals' manure and when they pass gas.

WATER VAPOR IN THE AIR CAN ALSO ACT AS A GREENHOUSE GAS.

Two other gases make up a small percentage of greenhouse gases. They are nitrous oxide and fluorides. Fluorides are used in refrigeration. Nitrous oxides mainly come from the fertilizers used on farms.

As people rely more and more on technology, more fossil fuels are used. But by burning more fossil fuels, we are releasing even more greenhouse gases into the air. These gases trap more heat in our atmosphere and cause climate change.

Chapter 3

OUR CLIMATE AFFECTS OUR AIR

When fossil fuels burn, they don't just give off greenhouse gases. They also pollute the air by adding ozone, dust, and other pollutants to the atmosphere. Air pollution is anything in the air that is harmful to humans or the environment. As our climate warms, air pollution will get worse.

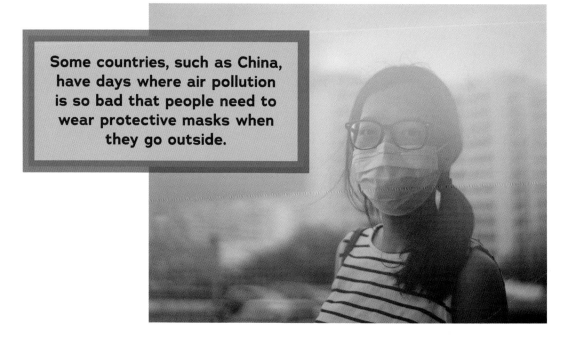

Some countries, such as China, have days where air pollution is so bad that people need to wear protective masks when they go outside.

Ozone

Ozone is one form of air pollution. It is a gas made of three oxygen atoms. Some ozone is good for us. This good ozone floats high in the top layer of our atmosphere. It shields Earth from the sun's ultraviolet rays. These rays can cause cancer and harm crops.

Good ozone cannot shield us from all the sun's ultraviolet rays. We use sunscreen to protect us from the rest.

But ozone is bad when it hovers near Earth's surface. A reaction between sunlight and the exhaust from burning fossil fuels creates this ozone. Ozone is a major ingredient in smog. Smog is a thick, dark haze formed by sunlight reacting with exhaust, smoke, and ozone.

Smog makes breathing difficult. It can even be deadly. The ozone in smog irritates the throat and lungs. It is particularly bad for people who are sick or have asthma. But even healthy people can have problems breathing when ozone levels are too high.

This air is filled with ozone and dust. If the air becomes more polluted, dark smog will form.

Acid rain from sulfur dioxide is deadly to trees. Over time, it can destroy a whole forest.

Sulfur Dioxide

Sulfur dioxide is a pollutant given off by burning fossil fuels in power plants and factories. It contains one sulfur atom and two oxygen atoms. Sulfur dioxide forms particles that can get deep into your lungs and damage them. Even brief exposure to sulfur dioxide can make it difficult to breathe.

Sulfur dioxide is also found in acid rain. Both nitrous oxide (a greenhouse gas) and sulfur dioxide can combine with water to form acid rain. When acid rain runs into lakes and streams, it can kill fish and other wildlife. Acid rain can eat away at buildings and monuments too.

All around the world, beautiful buildings and sculptures are ruined by acid rain.

IF SOIL GETS TOO DRY, DUST STORMS SUCH
AS THIS ONE IN 1936 ARE POSSIBLE.
DUST STORMS CAN BE DEADLY.

Dirt and Dust

Another type of air pollution is floating particles, such as dust or smoke. As climate change gets worse, some places experience drought. A drought is a long period of dryness. If soil is dry, the wind easily blows it away. This puts more dust into the air and makes it harder to breathe.

Drought also increases the risk of forest fires. When forests get too dry, they can catch fire. These fires create smoke. Smoke can give you a runny nose, make your eyes burn, and make you cough. Tiny particles of smoke can penetrate deep into your lungs, making it difficult to breathe. If you have heart or lung problems, smoke can make your symptoms worse.

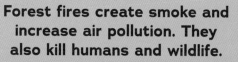

Forest fires create smoke and increase air pollution. They also kill humans and wildlife.

Like greenhouse gases, pollen
is impossible to see in the air. But
people with allergies react to it.

Climate change may also mean more pollen in the
air. Pollen is a tiny yellow grain produced by flowers to
fertilize their seeds. As Earth warms, plants will have
a longer growing season, so they will have more time
to produce pollen. Pollen is a problem for people with
allergies because it can make them sneeze and cough.
It can give them itchy eyes and skin.

MOLD GROWS IN WARM, DAMP ENVIRONMENTS.

Climate change may also increase indoor air pollution. As Earth warms, ice at the North Pole and South Pole melts. The sea level rises. Heat from higher temperatures also puts more energy in the atmosphere, which causes more violent storms. Storms and rising sea levels increase flooding. Buildings that have been flooded sometimes grow mold. Mold spores floating inside buildings can make people sick.

The good news is that many people are working to improve our air quality and slow down climate change.

STEM In Depth: The Air Quality Index

Each day, scientists take air samples from all over the United States. They use special devices to check the samples for ozone, dust, and other pollutants. They give a number rating the air's quality. It's called the Air Quality Index, or AQI. If the AQI is between 0 and 50, the air is fine. If the AQI is over 100, the air is harmful for people with breathing problems. If AQI is over 200, the air is very unhealthful for all people. You can find the AQI in your daily weather report.

See if you can find the AQI on a weather channel or app!

Chapter 4

IMPROVING OUR AIR QUALITY

Governments around the world are working hard to clean up our air. When a dangerous smog hit Pennsylvania in 1948 and London in 1952, thousands of people died and many became sick. The United States, Britain, and other countries passed laws to control air pollution to make sure the deadly smog didn't return. Thanks to these laws, the air is much cleaner now.

But even more is being done to improve our air quality and manage climate change. Nations are creating agreements to limit greenhouse gases. Some countries have switched from fossil fuels to renewable energy sources.

On December 12, 2015, world leaders in Paris reached an agreement for curbing climate change.

Renewable Energy

What is renewable energy, and why is it so important? Renewable energy comes from sources with unlimited energy, or energy that can never be used up. It also doesn't give off greenhouse gases. Some examples of renewable energy are wind power, solar power, waterpower, and geothermal power. Geothermal power comes from the heat stored in Earth. Scientists are working hard to find ways to use renewable energy more efficiently.

Wind turbines such as these generate electricity.

Many appliances such as washers and dryers are made in high-efficiency models. This means they use less energy.

Another way to lower greenhouse gases and reduce air pollution is to use less energy. When we burn less fuel, we put less carbon dioxide and pollution into our atmosphere. One way to use less energy is to use LED light bulbs instead of older, incandescent bulbs. LED bulbs use 90 percent less energy than incandescent bulbs. Some people also choose to drive more fuel-efficient cars. These burn less gasoline. Some even burn no gas at all.

Governments are also protecting their forests and planting trees in cities and towns. Trees take in carbon dioxide and give off oxygen. They also clean pollution particles from the air. In the United States, forests soak up between 10 and 20 percent of the country's carbon dioxide.

People are searching for new ways to combat climate change and improve our air quality. We are learning more about how greenhouse gases affect our planet. We are finding more efficient ways to generate energy. We are switching to renewable power sources that don't pollute our air. We are figuring out better ways to live with our changing climate.

Some cities are creating bike-friendly roads and paths so that more people can bike to work instead of drive.

STEM In Depth: Draining Carbon Dioxide

Scientists call forests carbon sinks. Trees and other plants clean carbon dioxide from the air. They take carbon dioxide into their leaves. Using energy from sunlight, they break off the carbon atom. Trees make sugar from the carbon atom. They use sugar for food and release the oxygen atoms back into the air. Humans and animals use that oxygen to breathe. An acre (0.4 ha) of forest can remove about 2.5 tons (2.3 t) of carbon from the air each year!

We can improve our air quality by protecting forests and planting new ones.

What You Can Do

- **Turn off the lights when you leave a room.** This cuts down on fossil fuel use.

- **When possible, walk or ride a bike instead of asking a parent to drive you places.** The less gas we burn, the better for Earth.

- **Put on a sweater instead of turning up the heat.** Furnaces run on fossil fuels, just as lights do.

- **Plant a tree or garden.** Think of green, growing things as natural sponges for carbon dioxide!

Climate Change Timeline

1860   Jean Joseph Etienne Lenoir invents an internal combustion engine, which runs on fossil fuel.

1948   Twenty people die and thousands are sickened in thick smog in Donora, Pennsylvania.

1952   Smog in London kills thousands of people.

1970   The Clean Air Act is passed in the United States.

2015   Almost two hundred countries sign the Paris Agreement to fight climate change.

2016   *Solar Impulse 2*, a solar powered airplane, completes a flight around the world.

Glossary

Air Quality Index: a measurement of the pollution in the air

carbon dioxide: the most abundant greenhouse gas in Earth's atmosphere

carbon sink: something such as a forest or an ocean that takes in more carbon dioxide than it gives off

climate change: a long-term change in Earth's weather patterns

fossil fuel: an energy source formed from the remains of prehistoric plants or animals

geothermal power: heat energy stored in Earth

greenhouse gas: a gas in the atmosphere that can trap heat from the sun

internal combustion engine: a motor that works by burning fuel inside it

methane: a greenhouse gas that is about twenty-five times stronger at warming the air than carbon dioxide is

ozone: a gas made of three oxygen atoms

renewable energy: a source of energy that isn't used up but, instead, is naturally replaced, such as energy from the sun or wind

Learn More about Air Quality

Books

Lawrence, Ellen. *Dirty Air*. New York: Bearport, 2014. Read more about how burning fossil fuels pollutes our air.

MacAulay, Kelley. *Why Do We Need Air?* New York: Crabtree, 2014. Find out why it's important for our health and our planet to have clean air.

Wang, Andrea. *How Can We Reduce Fossil Fuel Pollution?* Minneapolis: Lerner Publications, 2016. Learn more about how we can reduce air pollution.

Websites

Kids' Crossing: Living in the Greenhouse!
http://eo.ucar.edu/kids/green/index.htm
Explore climate change with pictures, infographics, and games on this fun website.

NASA Climate Kids: What Is the Greenhouse Effect?
https://climatekids.nasa.gov/greenhouse-effect/
Videos, games, and activities found on this website teach kids all about climate change.

Tiki the Penguin: What You Can Do
http://tiki.oneworld.org/pollution/pollution10.html
Learn all about what you can do to make Earth a healthier, cleaner place to live.

Index

Photo Acknowledgments

Image credits: Science Museum/SSPL/NMPFT/Daily Herald Archive/agency/Getty Images, p. 4; Caiaimage/Andy Roberts/Riser/Getty Images, p. 5; AFP/Getty Images, p. 6; Image Source/Getty Images, p. 7; Portland Press Herald/Maine Sunday Telegram/Getty Images, p. 8; Petar Mulaj/iStock/Getty Images, p. 9; Harvey Schwartz/Photolibrary/Getty Images, p. 10; Peter Cade/The Image Bank/Getty Images, p. 11; Colleen Gara/Moment/Getty Images, p. 12; d3sign/Moment/Getty Images, p. 13; Bet_Noire/iStock/Getty Images, p. 14; Beata Zawrzel/NurPhoto/Getty Images, p. 15; xxmmxx/iStock/Getty Images, p. 16; jacquesvandinteren/iStock/Getty Images, p. 17; Universal History Archive/UI/Getty Images, p. 18; Daryl Pederson/First Light/Getty Images, p. 19; Frank Bienewald/LightRocket/Getty Images, p. 20; John_vlahidis/iStock/Getty Images, p. 21; CHIH YUAN Ronnie Wu/Alamy Stock Photo, p. 22; NurPhoto/NurPhoto/Getty Images, p. 23; Maria Wachala/Moment/Getty Images, p. 24; Sidekick/E+/Getty Images, p. 25; Topic Images/Getty Images, p. 26; Brazil Photos/LightRocket/Getty Images, p. 27.

Cover: Dennis Macdonald/Photolibrary/Getty Images